You'll Live Again

Collages by Fifer Horwitz

You'll Live Again

For information about this title or to order other books and/or electronic media, contact the publisher:

Book Architecture

One Richmond Square, Suite 112K

Providence, RI 02906

YoullLiveAgain.com

Fifer@ YoullLiveAgain.com

ISBN: 978-0-9864204-4-3

Printed in the United States of America

Cover and Interior design: 1106 Design

Table of Contents

Artist's Statement

I got this box of postcards for Christmas one year, and I didn't know what to do with them. I wanted to collage one day, and I thought it would be cool to use these. I didn't want to use technology; I didn't want to read; I wanted to be productive but I didn't want to know ahead of time what I was going to produce.

Art doesn't really have a reason, in terms of being something specific to accomplish. Now that I'm done, I can see certain themes: pacifism, being a teenager ... I shouldn't even tell you what they are. Because one of those themes is people who take themselves too seriously, so if I prove that by drawing your attention to manly men drinking beers or faded beauty queens, I'll be doing the same thing I say I don't like.

I would rather that you discover what there is in here for you, the same way that I like to discover a stash of magazines in a secondhand store in Brooklyn where you can have each one for a quarter. I never open them until I am out of the store because you only get that feeling once.

Will we live again? It would be cool to think that we do. When I look at the cover I see someone who's in a bad place ... kind of falling ... those difficult feelings can be turned around. The title can also apply to the repurposing of materials in the act of collage.

But, again, I may not have to say any of these things. Art is a safe place for me to express myself, and I want you to feel the same safety to think anything you want.

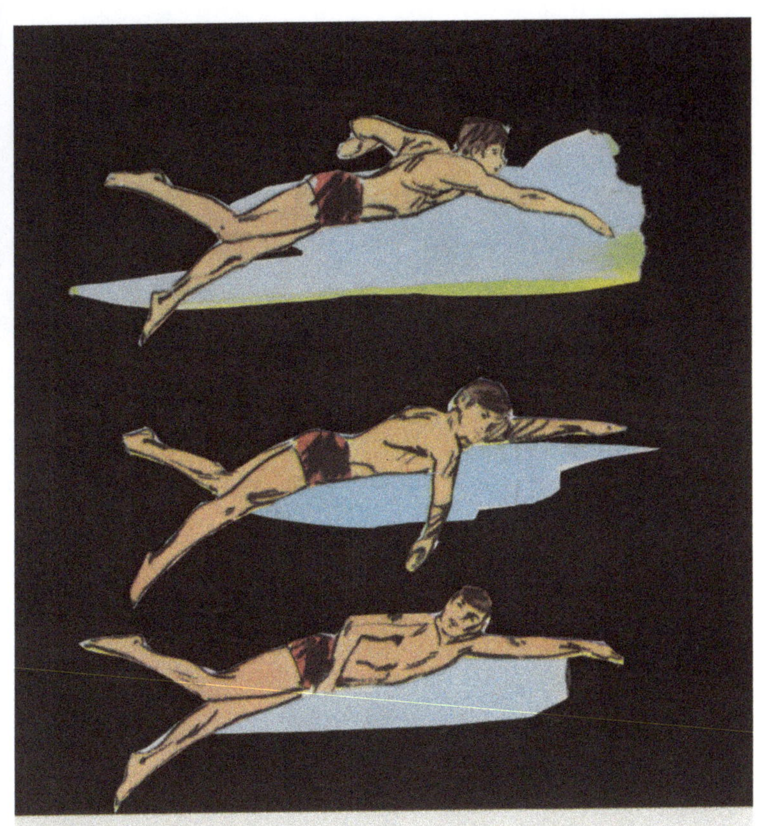

PANTONE® 19-4305
Pirate Black

Pirate Black

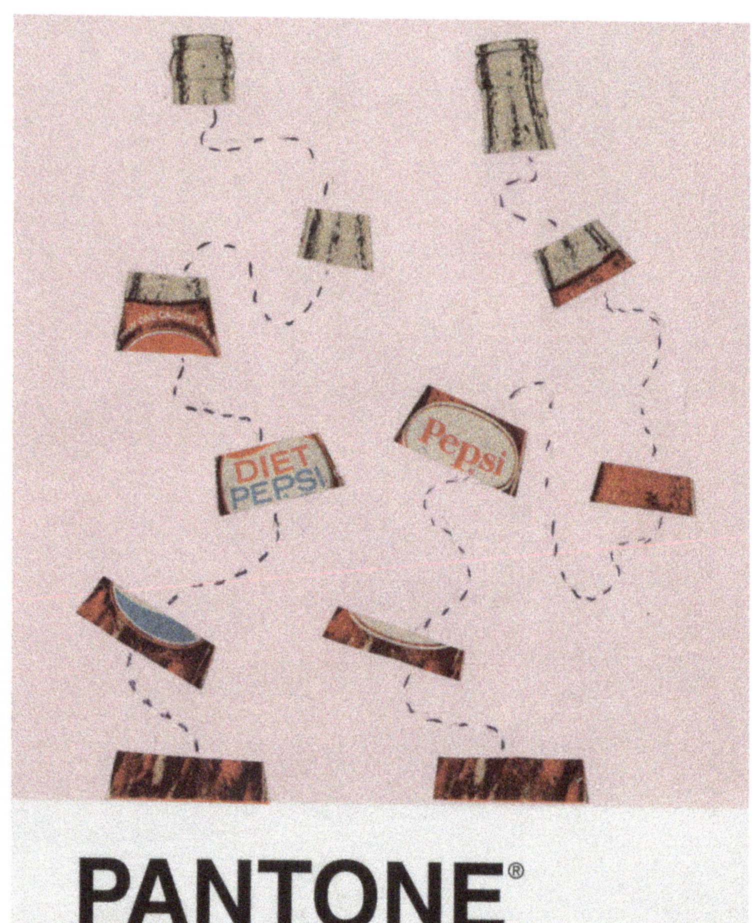

**PANTONE®
691**

Pour Here, I

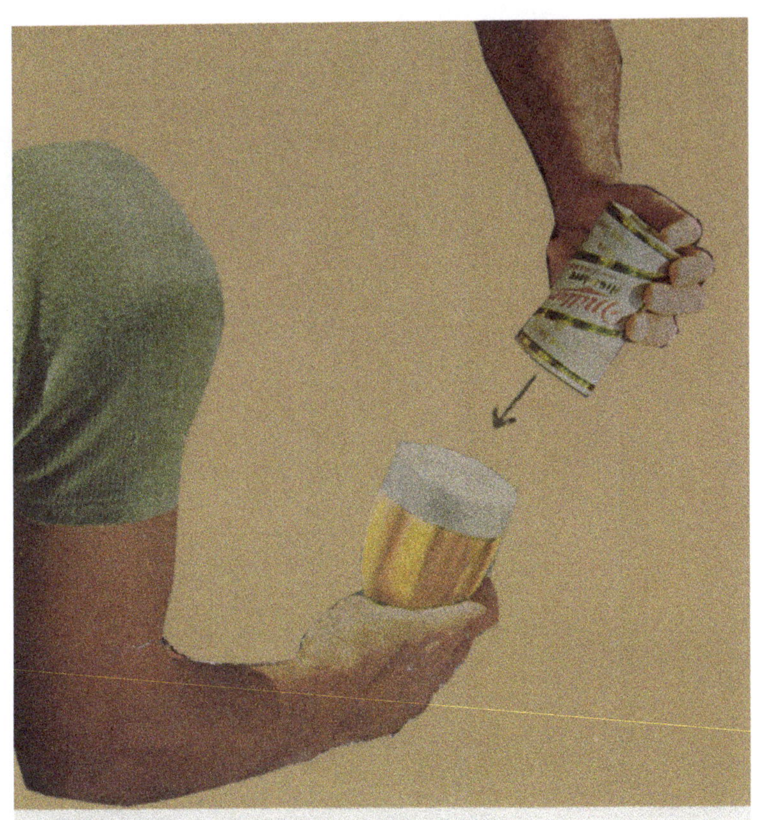

Pour Here, II

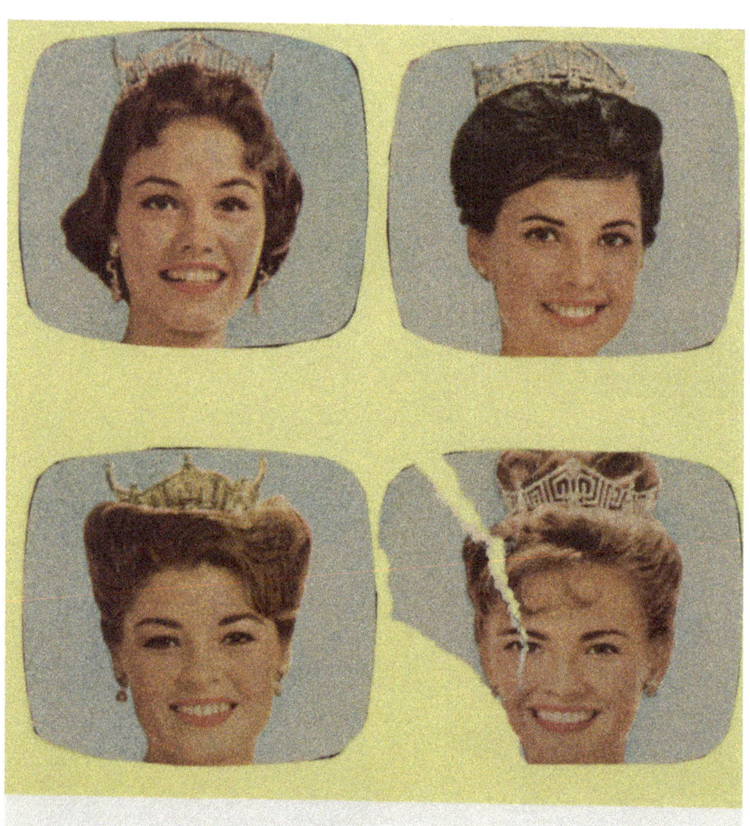

Beauty Queens Never Fade

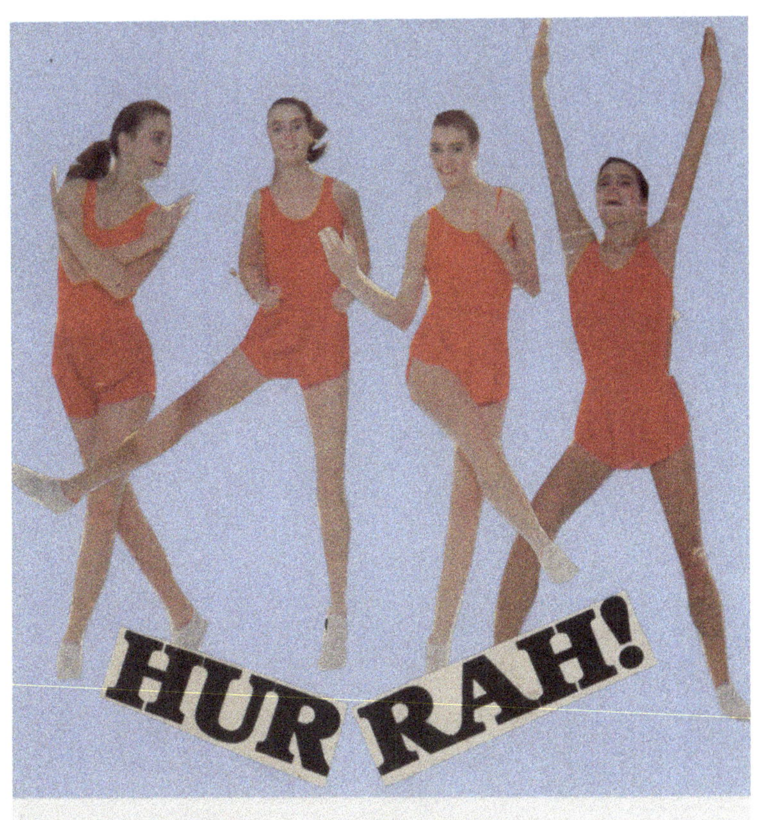

Hurrah!

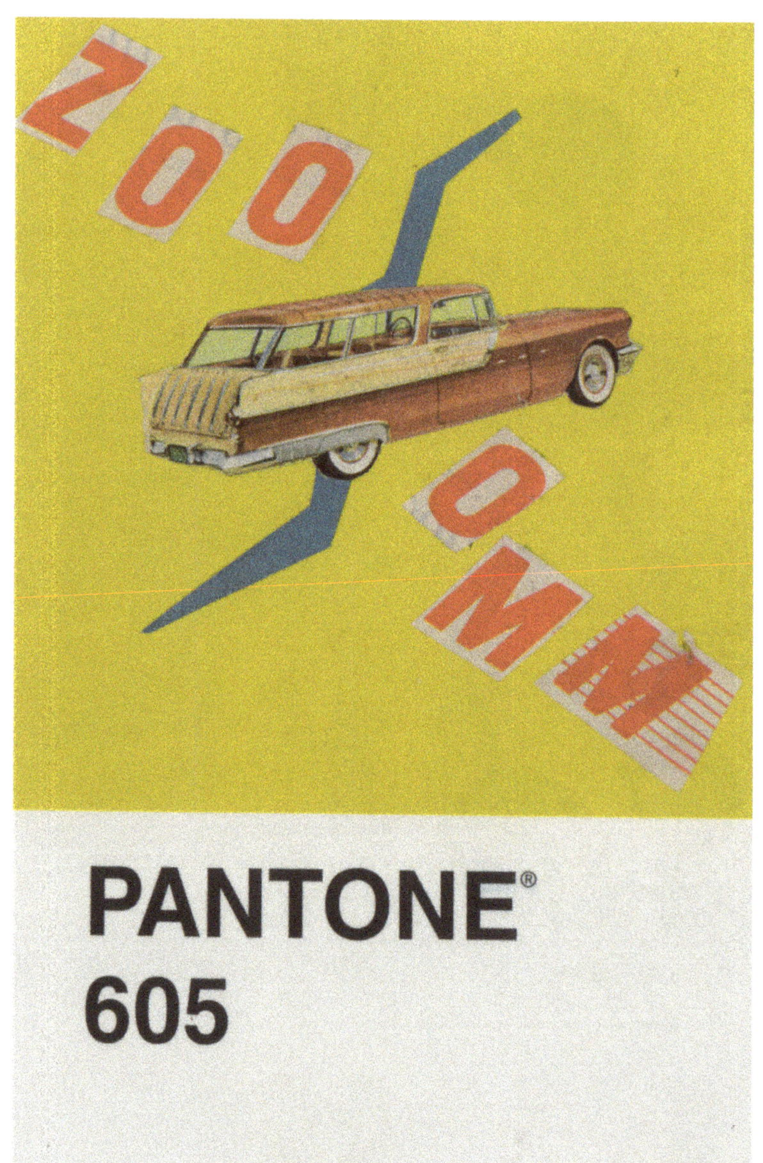

PANTONE®
605

Zoom

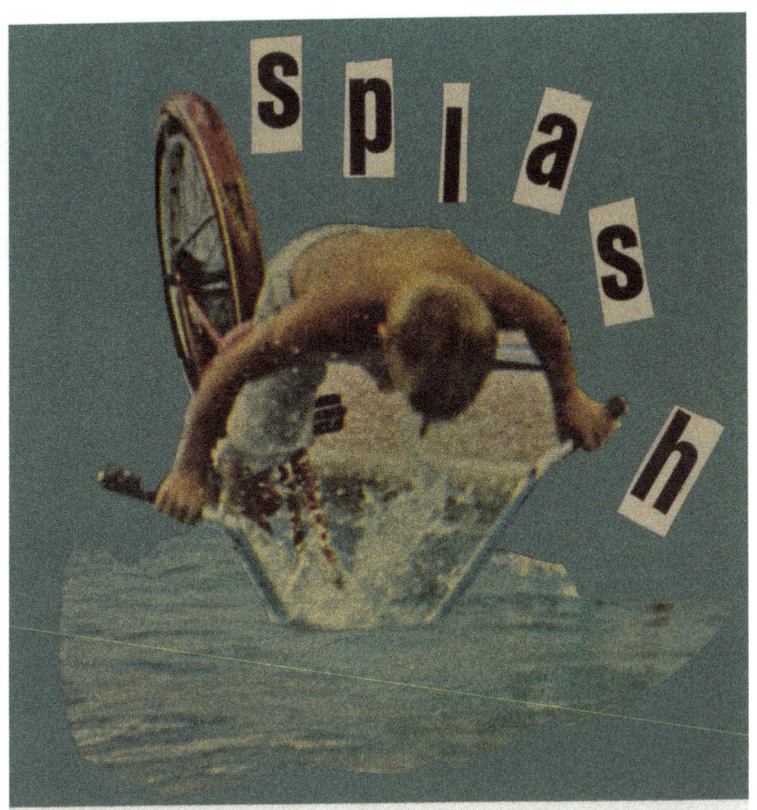

Splash

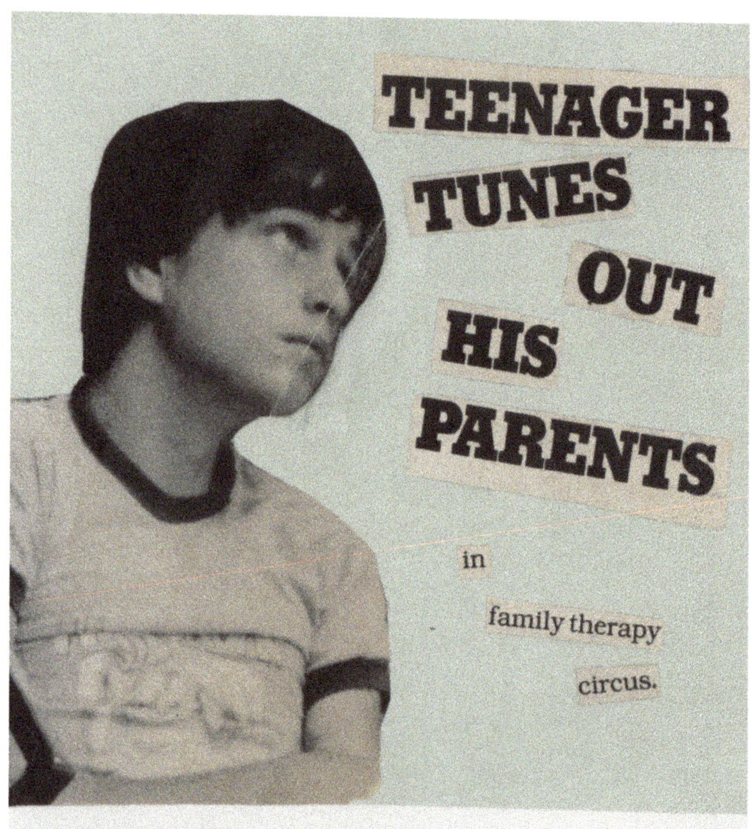

Family Circus

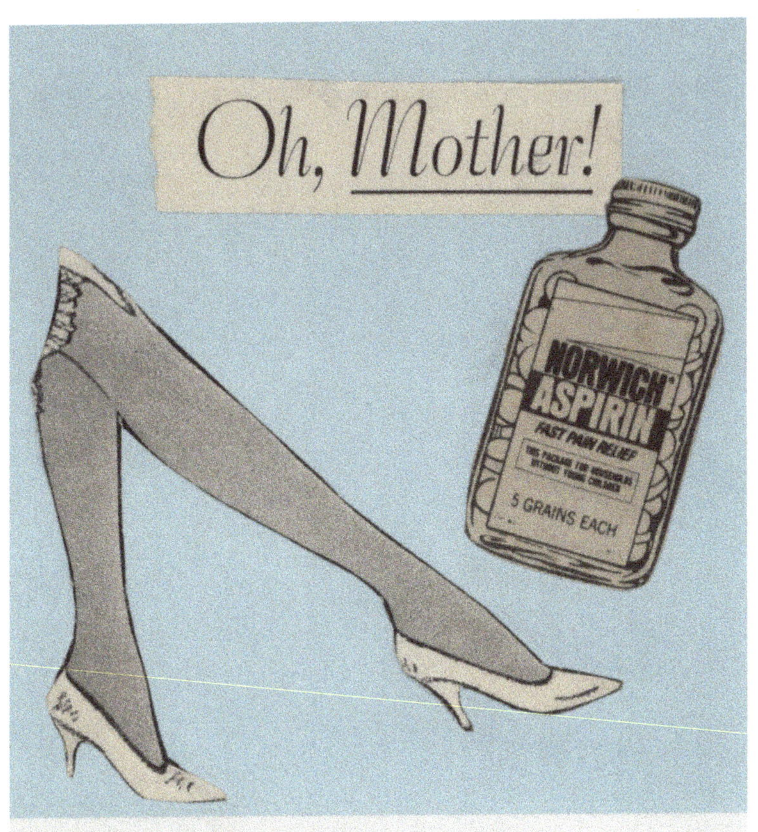

PANTONE®

635

Oh, Mother!

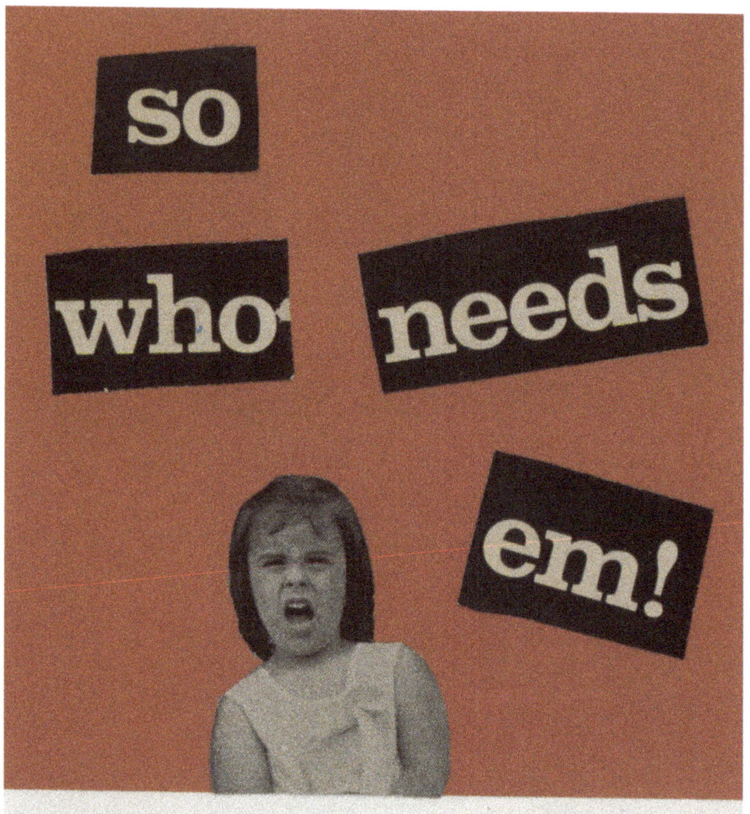

Who Needs Em!

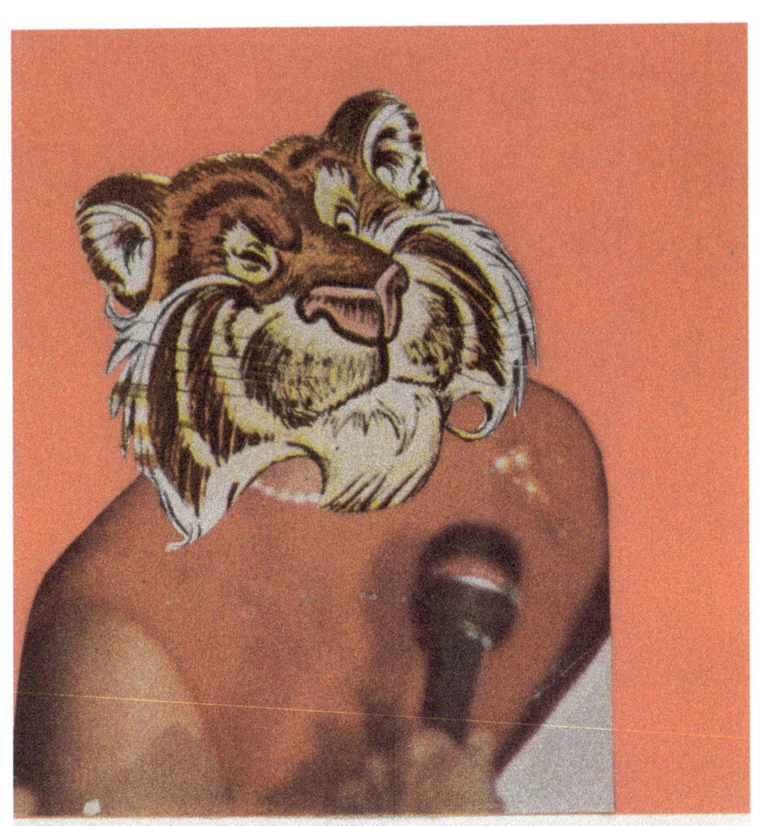

PANTONE® 17-1456

Tigerlily

Tigerlily

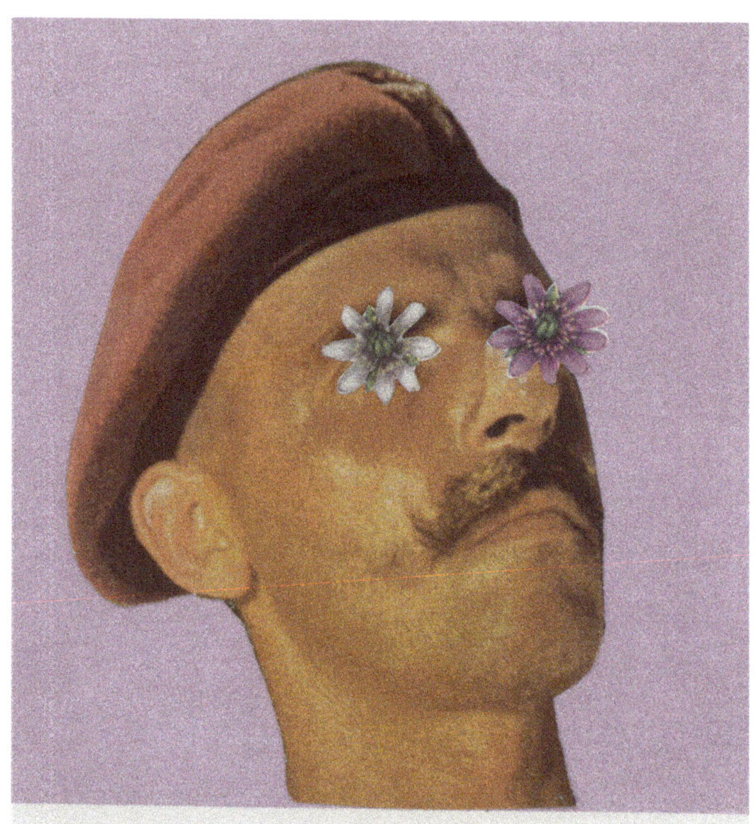

PANTONE® 14-3612
Orchid Bloom

Orchid Bloom

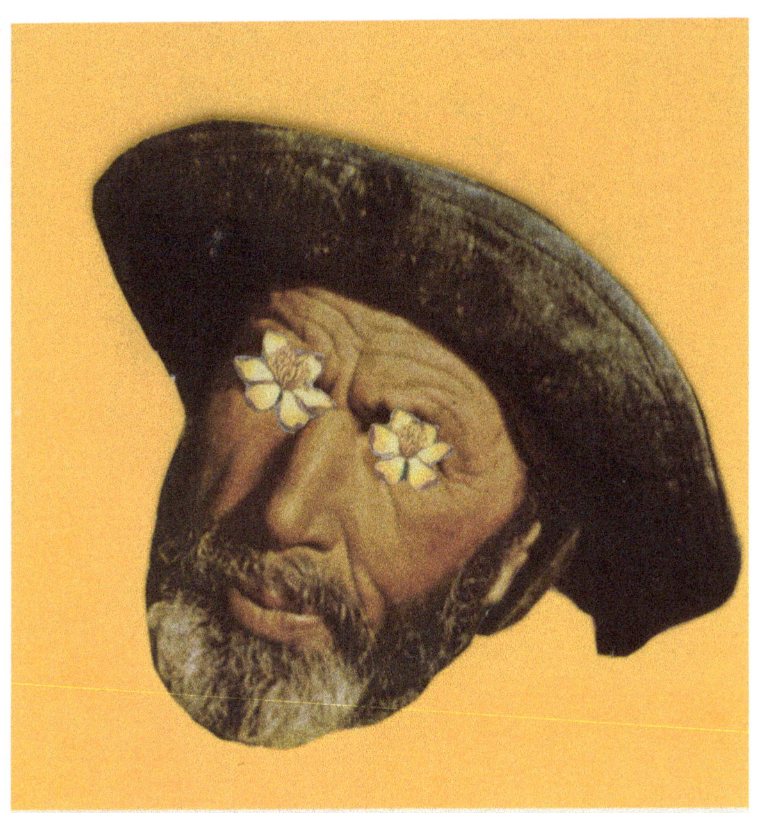

PANTONE®
142

Vaquero

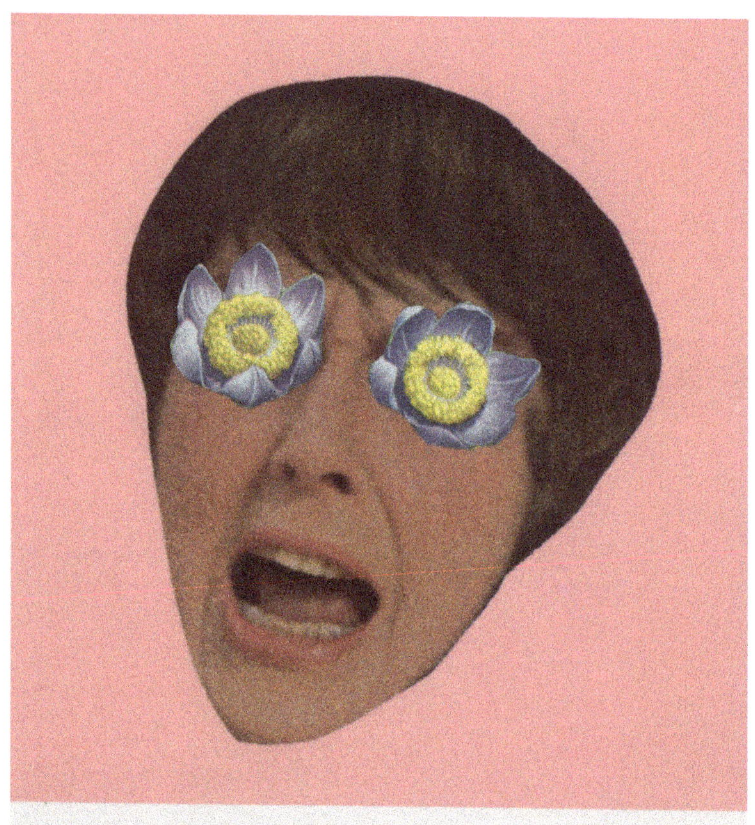

Peony

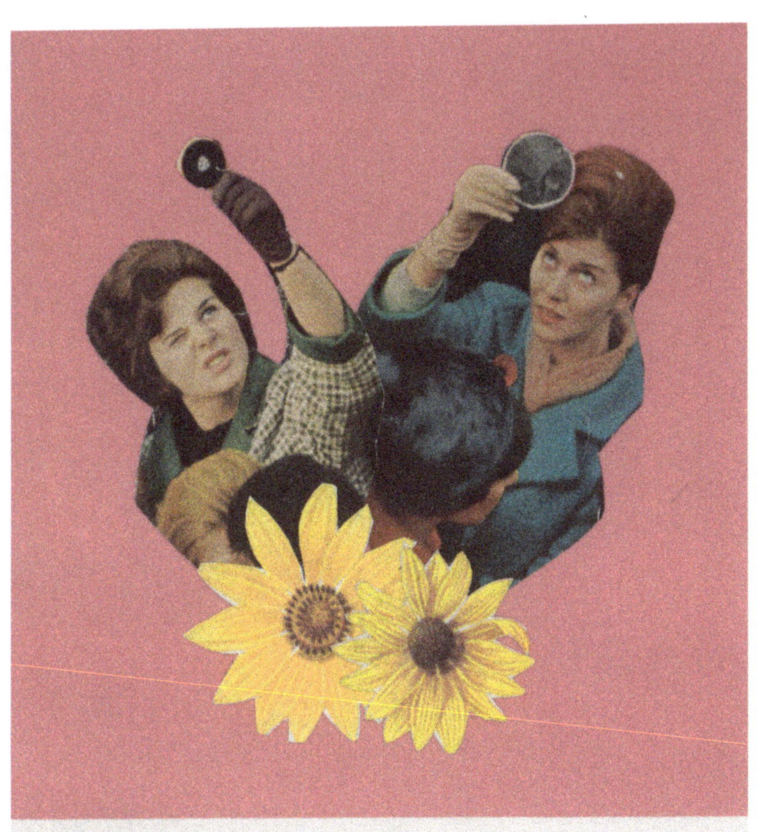

PANTONE®
493

Black-Eyed Susan

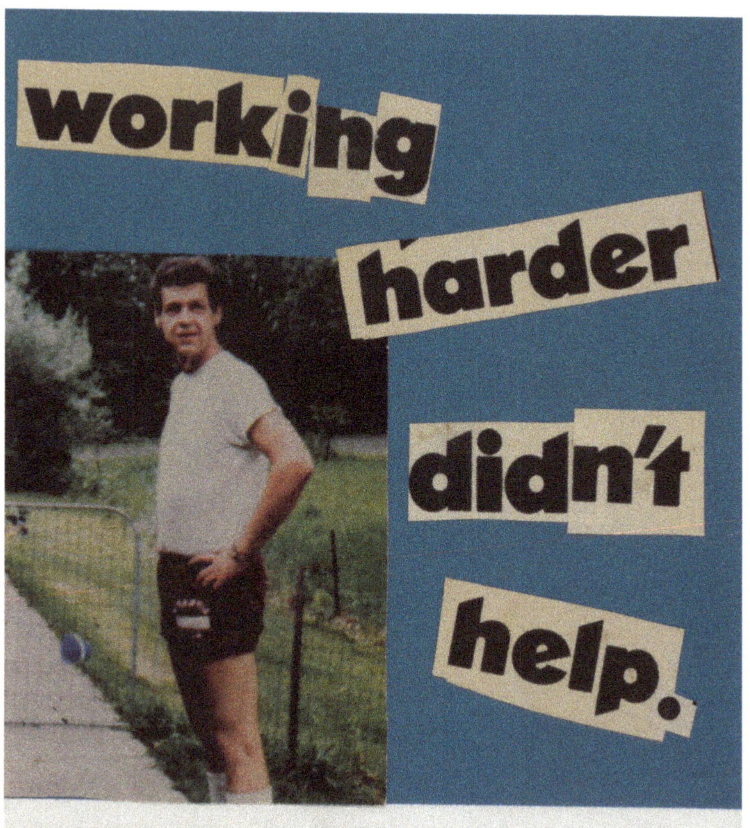

Working Harder Didn't Help

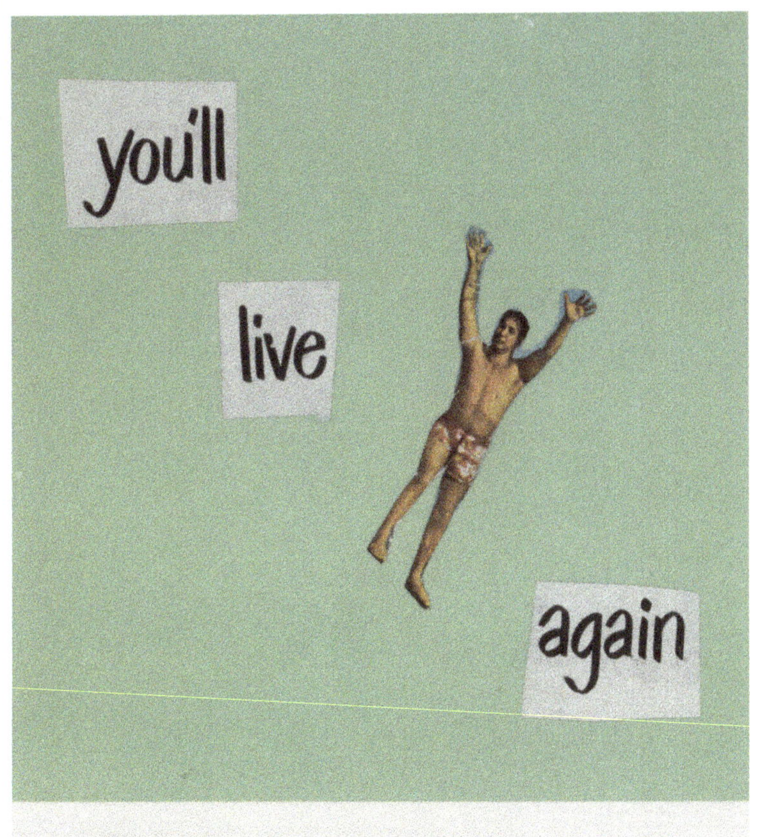

You'll Live Again

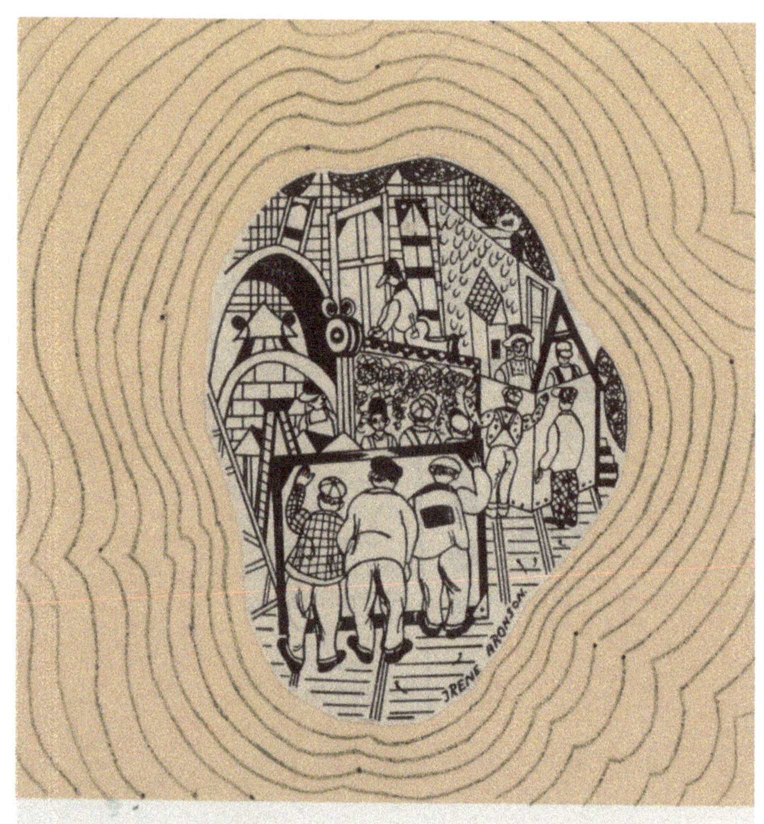

PANTONE® 14-1119
Winter Wheat

Winter Wheat

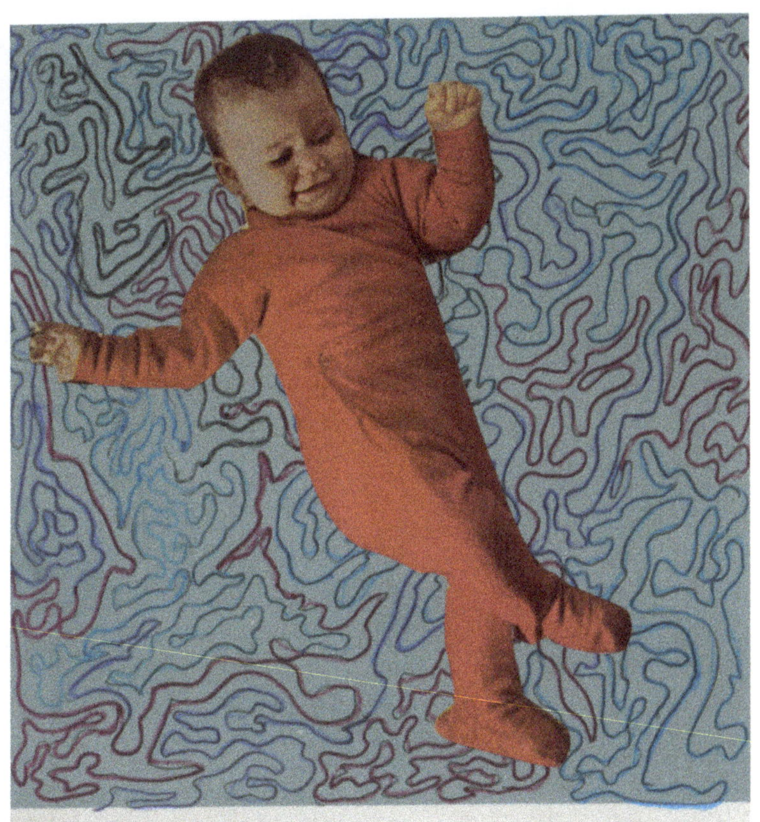

PANTONE® 15-5210

Nile Blue

Stimuli

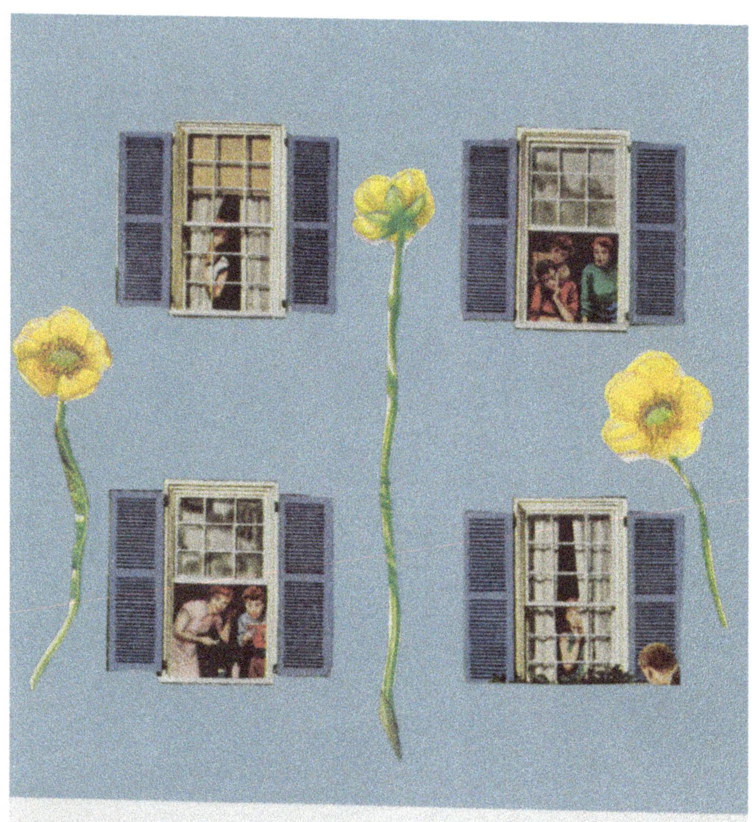

PANTONE® 14-4516
Petit four

Petit Four

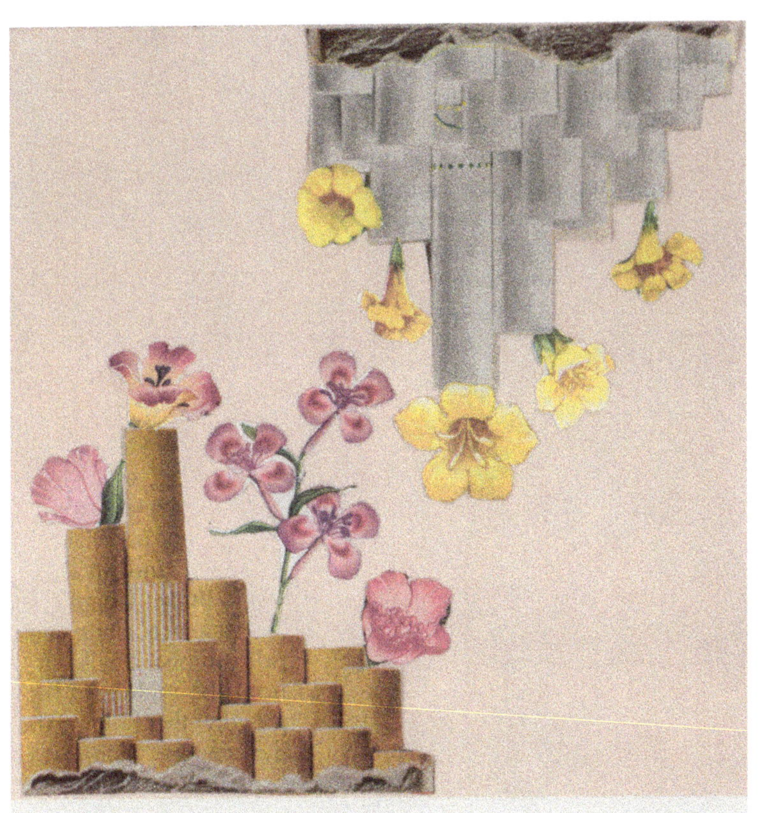

Untitled

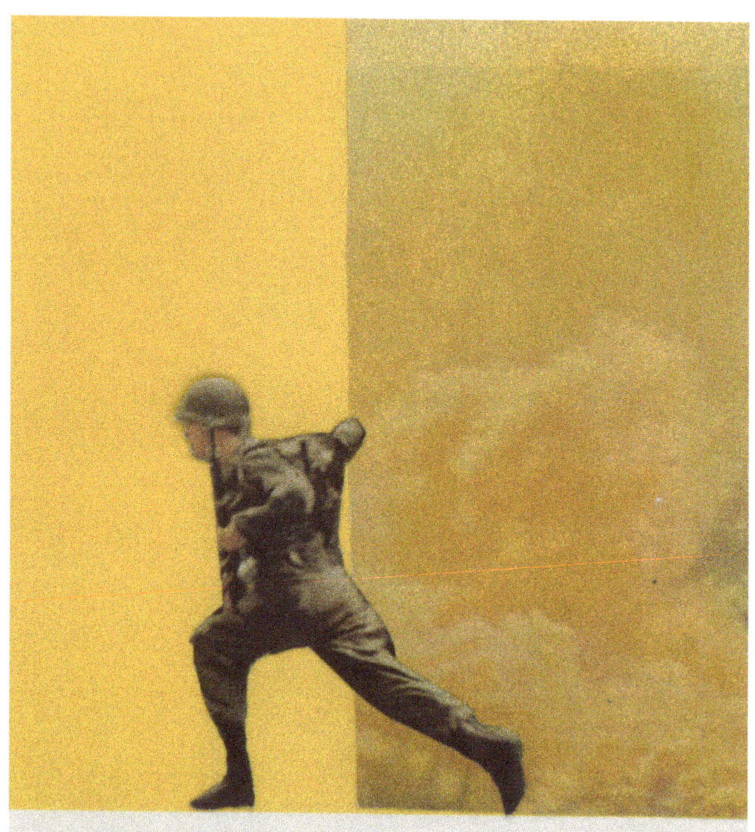

PANTONE® 14-0848
Mimosa

Ashes to Ashes

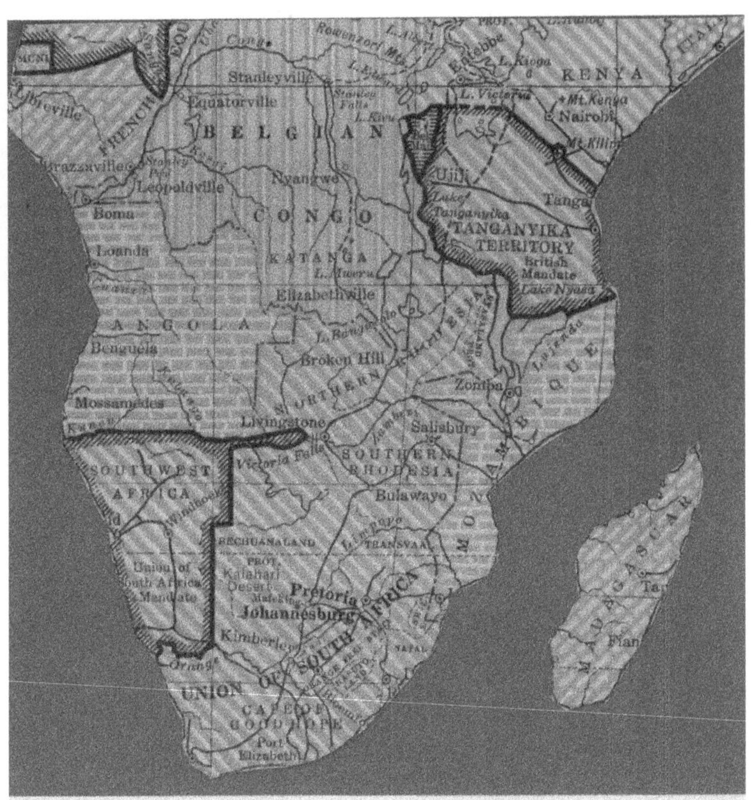

PANTONE®
7726

Cape of Good Hope

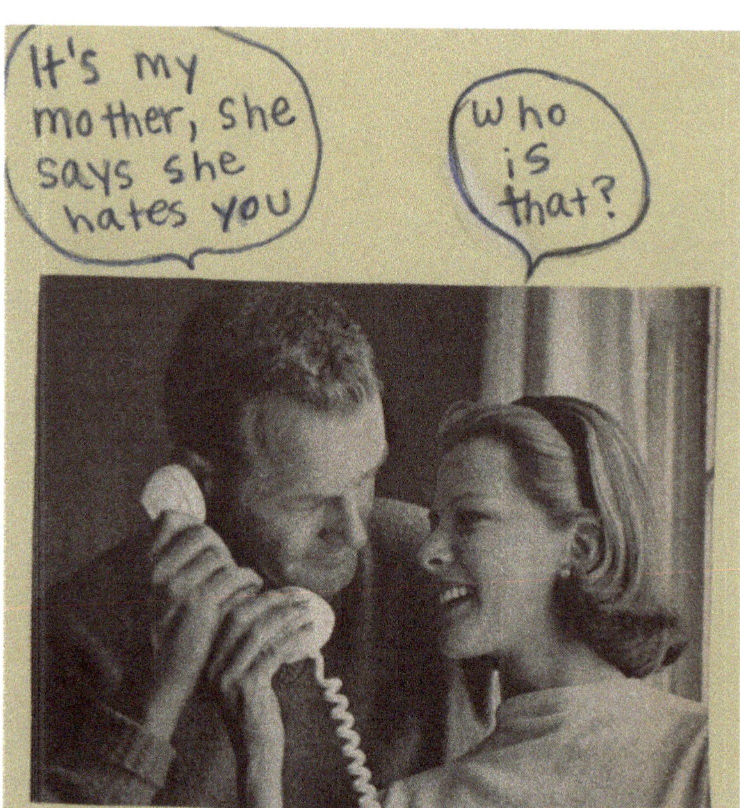

PANTONE®

4545

Who is That?

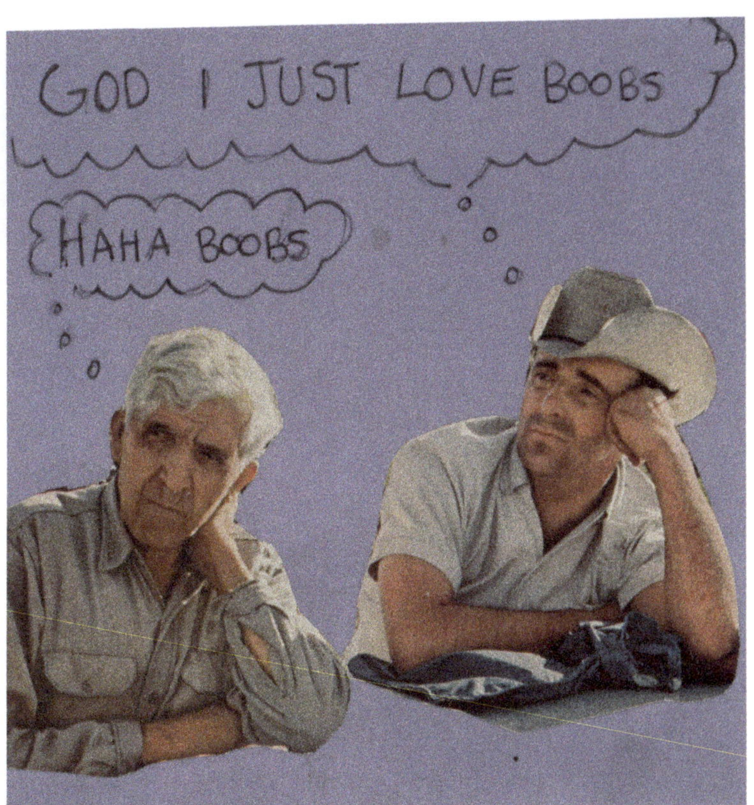

Boobs

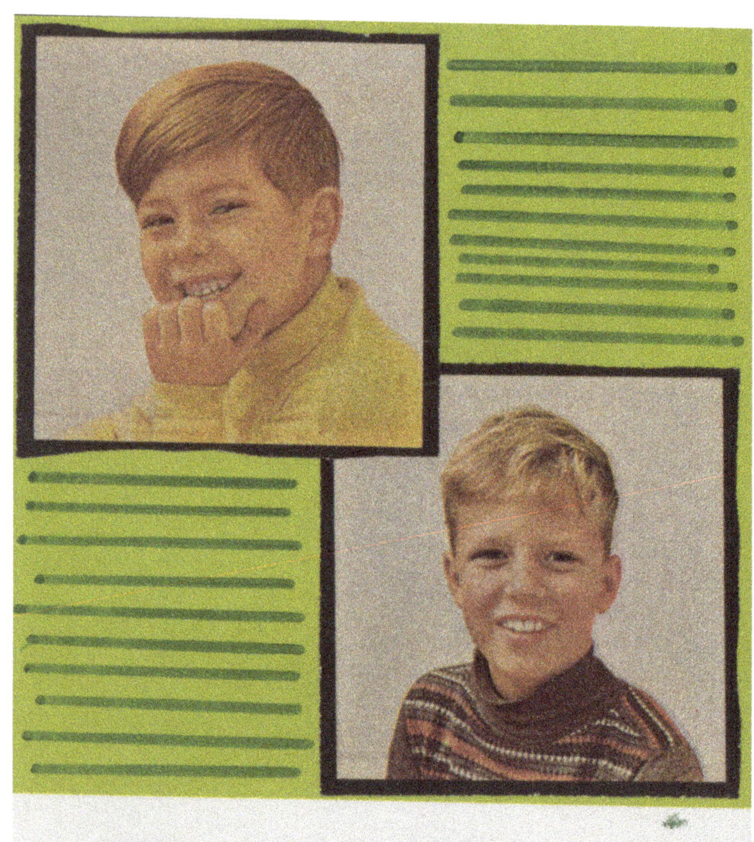

PANTONE®
583

Cheeky Lads

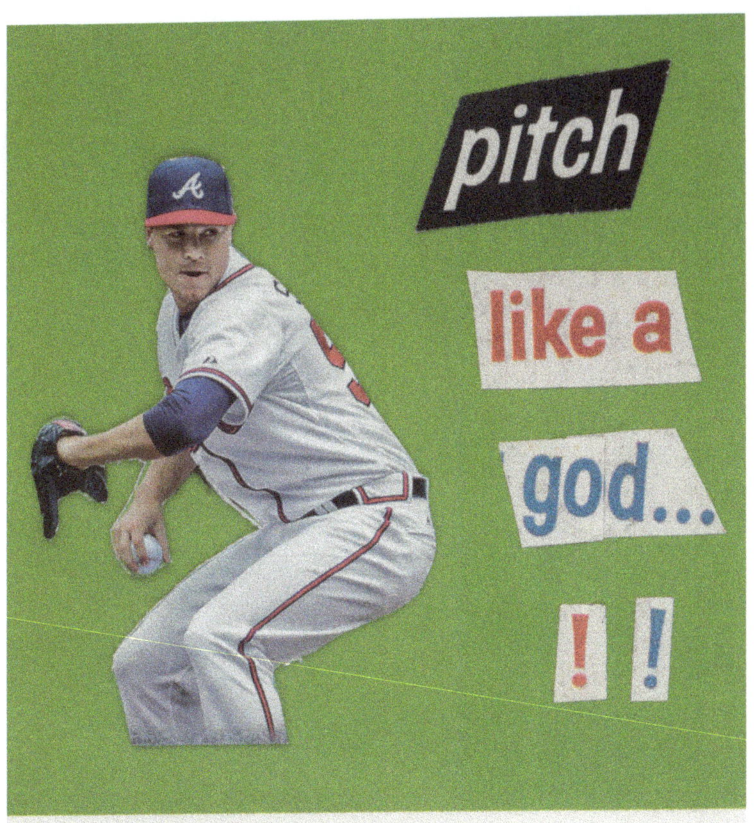

PANTONE®
7737

Pitch Like A God

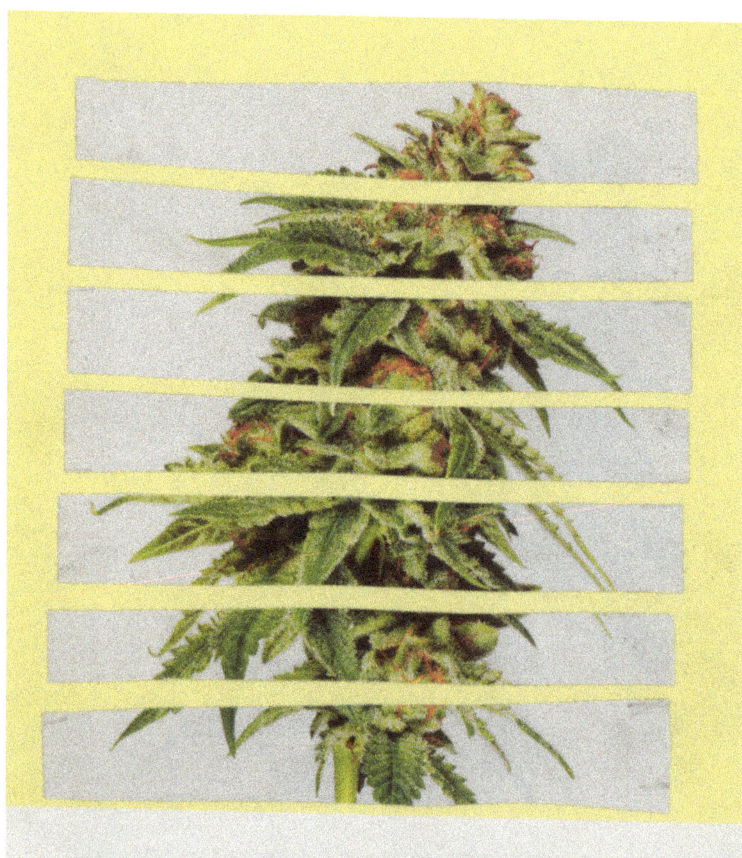

PANTONE®
600

Semi-Legal

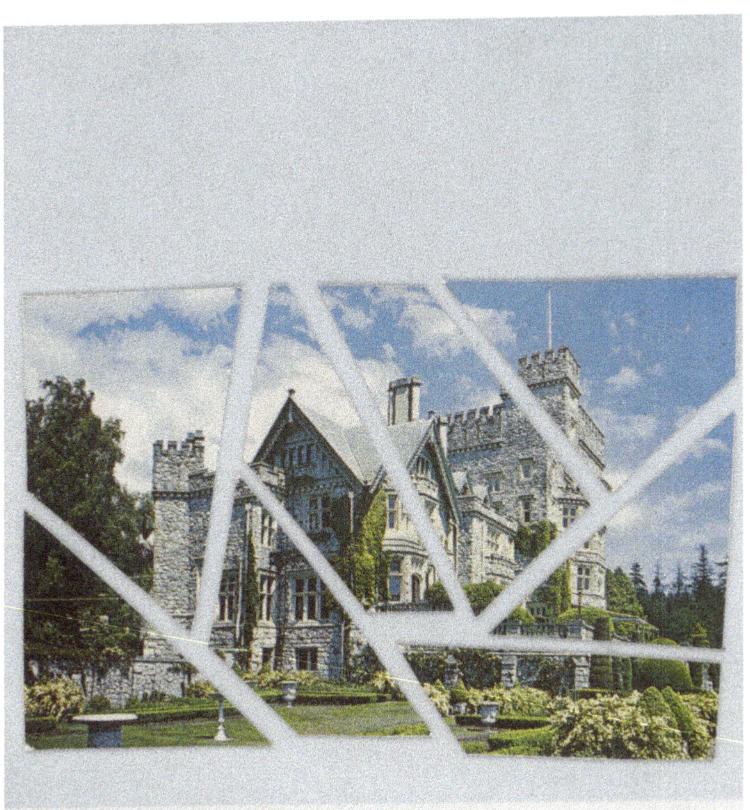

PANTONE®
656

Heading East

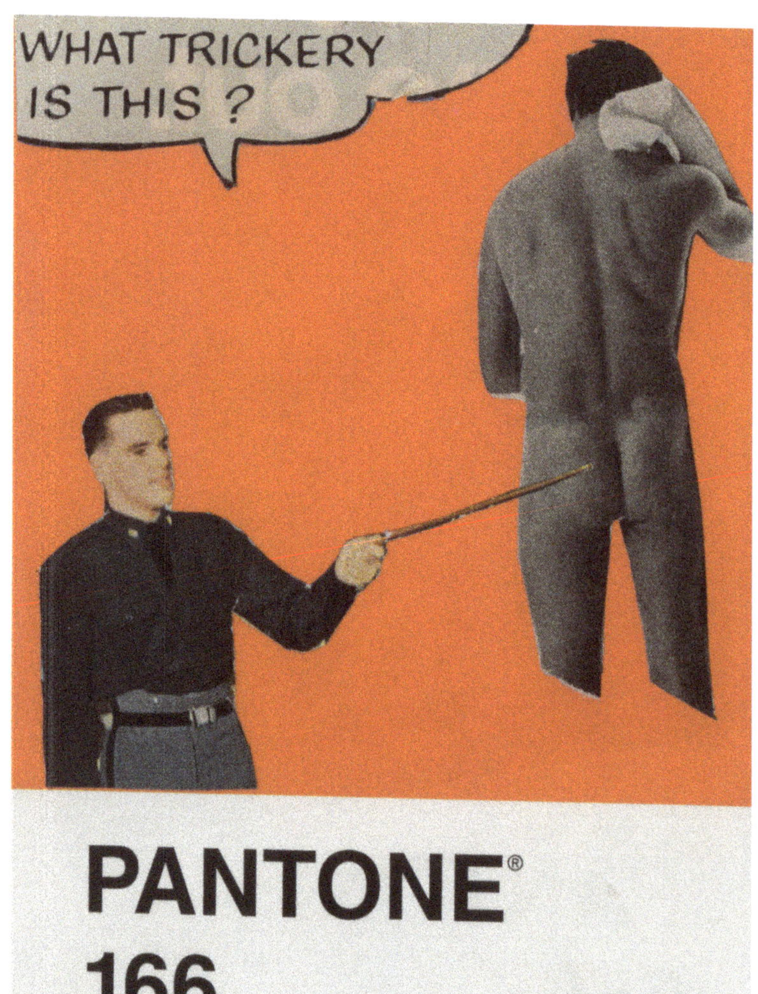

What Trickery Is This?

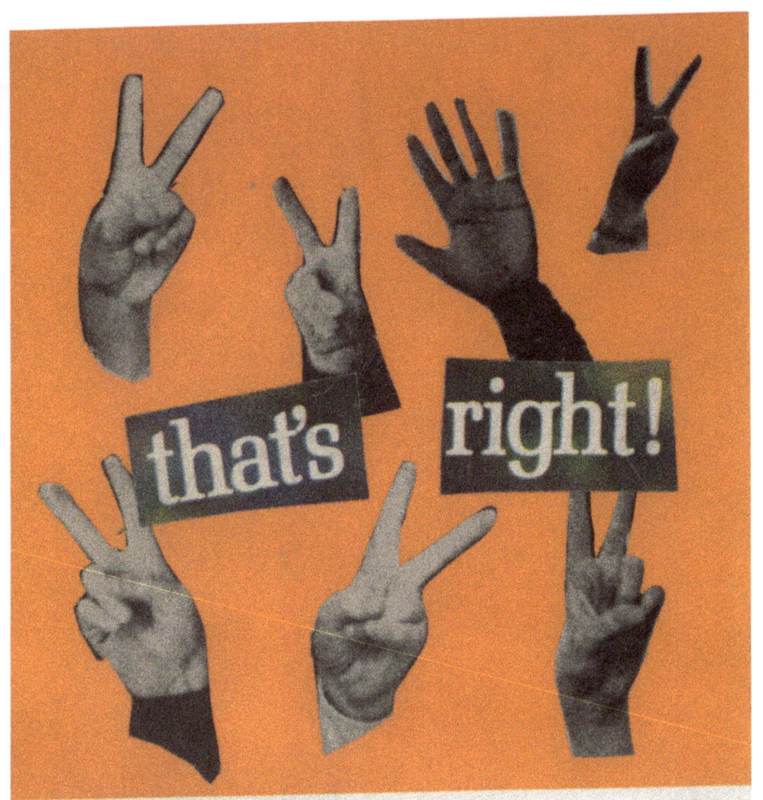

That's Right!

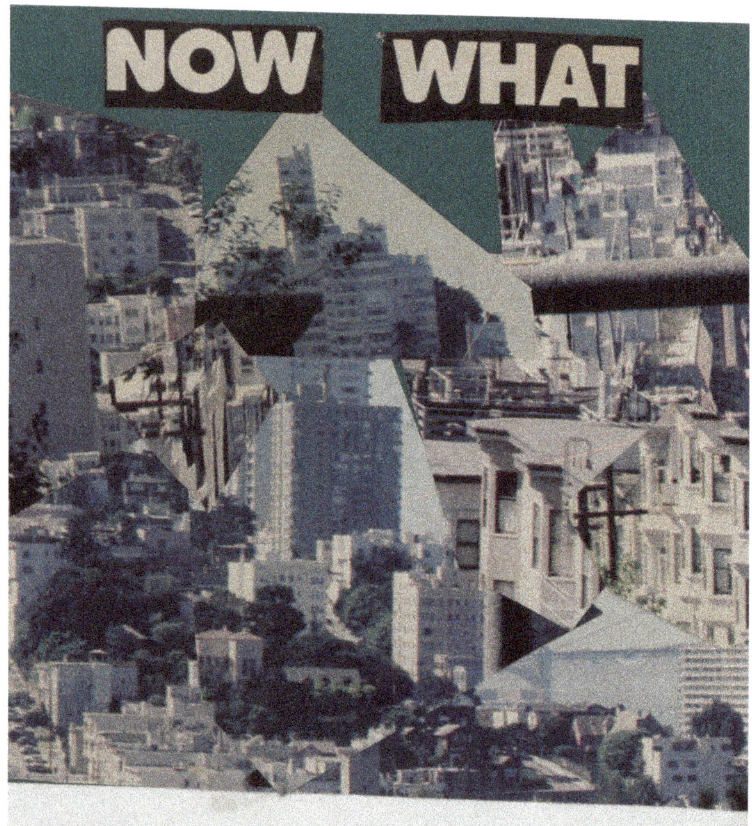

Now What

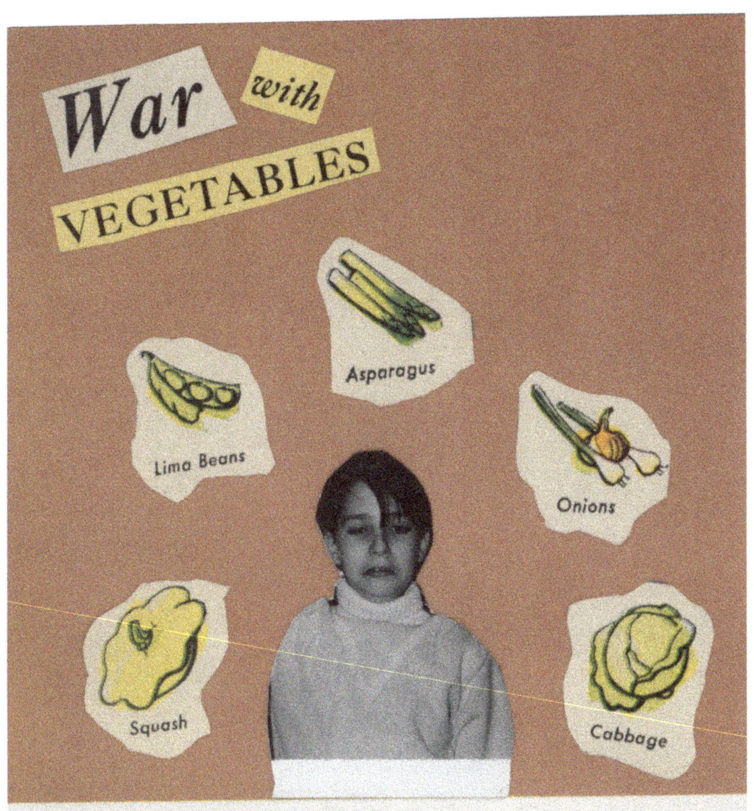

War With Vegetables

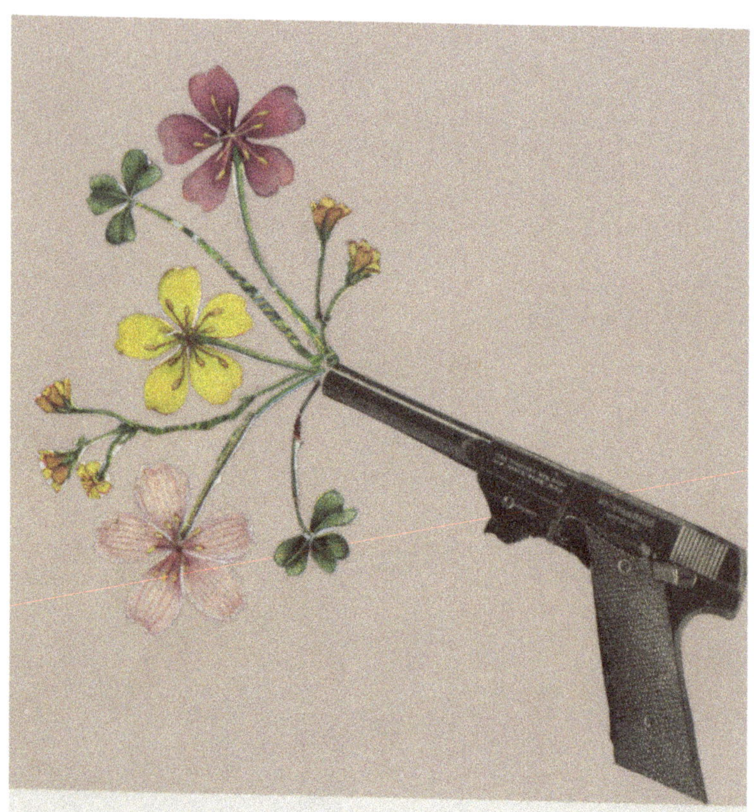

Whisper Pink

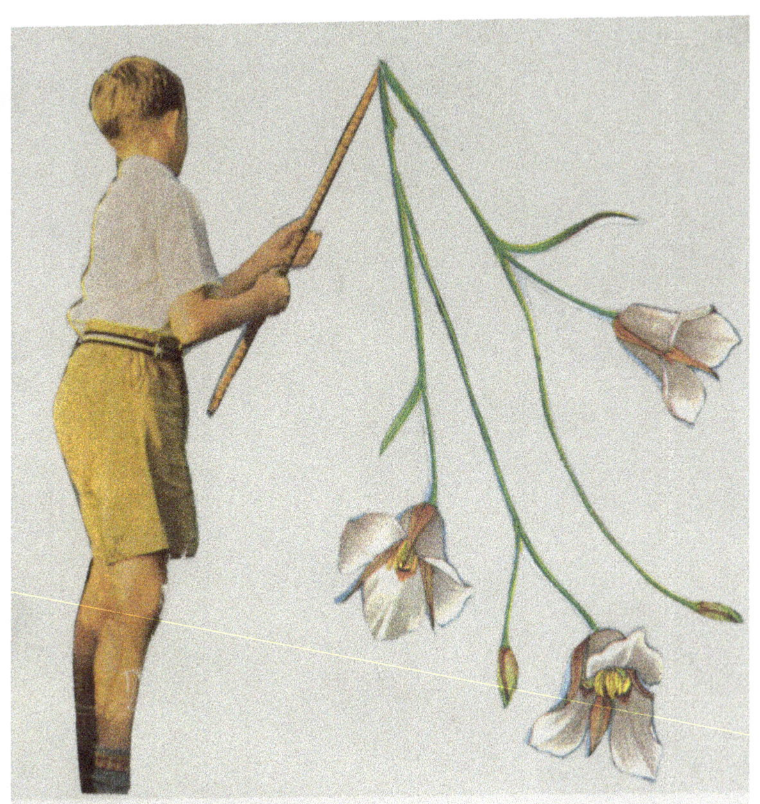

PANTONE® 11-4804
Lightest Sky

Lightest Sky

About the Artist

Fifer Horwitz was born in San Francisco, from where she claims her Type B heritage. She is now 17 years old and lives in Providence where you can see creativity on every corner. You can find her hanging out on Thayer street at Nice Slice but not Antonio's — Nice Slice has better pizza and better art.

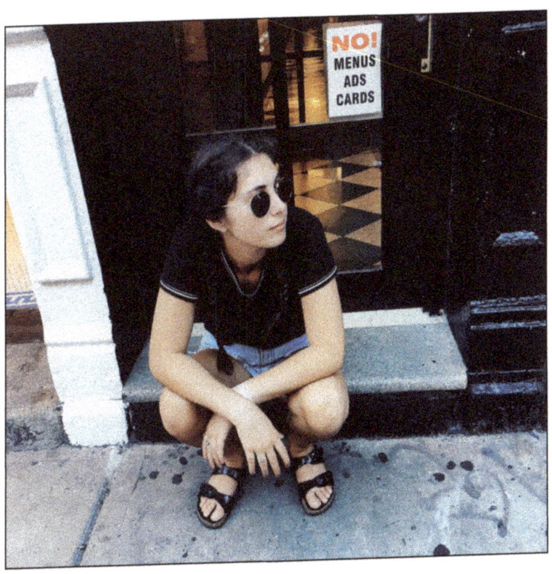

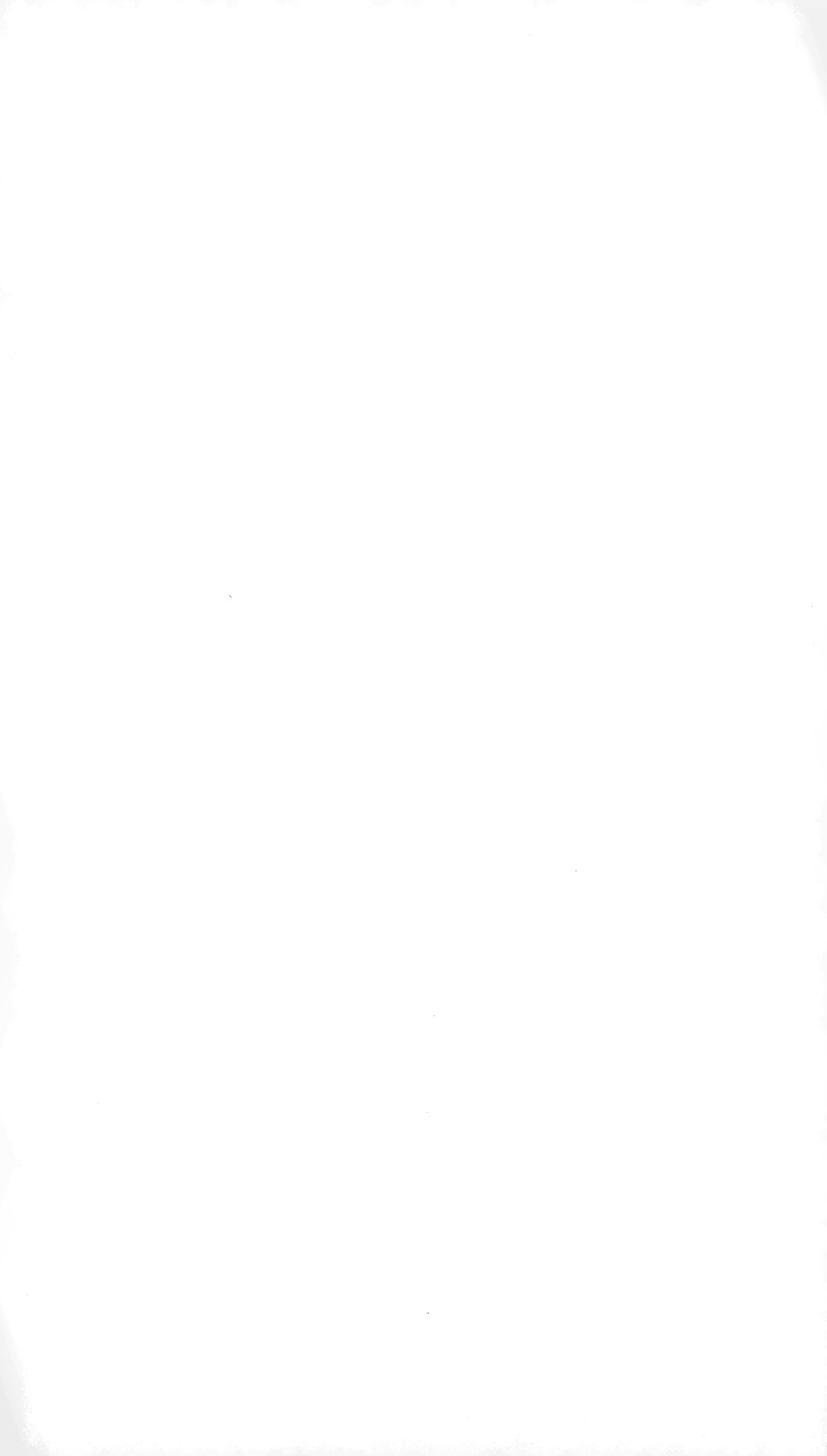